# I want to
# MAKE MOVIES

**PowerKiDS** press

New York

*Dedicated to my sister, my first movie buddy*

Published in 2009 by The Rosen Publishing Group, Inc.
29 East 21st Street, New York, NY 10010

First Edition

Editor: Amelie von Zumbusch
Book Design: Ginny Chu
Layout Design: Julio Gil
Photo Researcher: Jessica Gerweck

Photo Credits: Cover, p. 20 © AFP/Getty Images; pp. 4, 6, 8, 10, 12, 14, 16, 18 © Getty Images.

Library of Congress Cataloging-in-Publication Data

Dunn, Mary R.
  I want to make movies / Mary R. Dunn. — 1st ed.
      p. cm. — (Dream jobs)
  Includes index.
  ISBN 978-1-4042-4473-3 (library binding)
  1. Motion pictures—Juvenile literature.  I. Title.
  PN1994.5.D86 2009
  791.43—dc22
                                    2008000994

Manufactured in the United States of America

# Contents

The crew of the movie *Spider-Man* used cables, or ropes, to make the characters seem to fly through the air.

4

# A Crew of Workers

Have you ever noticed the long list of names that appears on the screen at the end of a movie? All those people played important parts in making that movie!

It takes many people working together to make a movie. For example, producers find the story and the money to make a movie. Actors play the characters. Directors **create** the overall look of a movie and guide the actors. Artists make drawings for props, or objects actors use. Other highly trained people supply **sound effects** and music for the movie.

*Enchanted* is a movie about a fairy-tale princess who finds herself in New York City. The movie uses dancing and singing to tell its story.

# A Story Comes to Life

Movies offer a great way to tell stories. Although people told stories for thousands of years before movies were invented, movies can use many tools, such as **special effects**, music, acting, and words to bring stories to life.

Moviegoers meet in darkened movie **theaters** to watch the magic of stories unfold on the lighted screen. As viewers watch and listen to a movie, they feel as if they are part of the story, too. Viewers laugh and sometimes cry as they are pulled into the world of the movie.

The movie *Star Wars*, seen here, is the first of several *Star Wars* movies written and directed by George Lucas.

# All Kinds of Movies

There are many genres, or kinds, of movies. Funny stories, called comedies, make us laugh. For example, *Shrek* tells of an ogre, or monster, who finds true love. *Underdog*, another comedy, is about a talking hound that helps the people of Capital City.

More than half of the 10 most successful kids' movies ever are science fiction movies. These movies generally tell about different worlds. For example, the movie *Star Wars* takes place "in a **galaxy** far, far away." In *E.T.: The Extra-Terrestrial*, a lost **alien** from another world finds his way home.

Screenwriter Michael Arndt won an honor called the Academy Award for writing the screenplay for the movie *Little Miss Sunshine*.

# Writing the Story

People called screenwriters most often make up the characters and plot, or story line, for a movie. Screenwriters then write screenplays, which have the words the actors will say and a description of some of their actions. Screenwriters get ideas from many places. Some screenplays are even based on real-life **events**.

Other movies' screenplays are based on books or **comics**. The book *Bridge to Terabithia* was made into a movie. It tells about friends who create an imaginary world. The movie *Spider-Man* is based on a well-known comic-book superhero.

Director Tony Scott, in the red hat, filmed parts of the movie *Man on Fire* in Mexico City, Mexico.

# Filming a Movie

Directors bring their own ideas to a screenplay. They guide and shape everything about a movie. Directors are in charge of a movie's set, or the place where a movie is made. Directors tell actors what to do and decide how to set up scenes. They oversee everyone working on a movie.

Directors work closely with **cinematographers**, the people in charge of the cameras. Cameras are tools used for recording scenes on **film**. Cinematographers decide how much light they will need, what kind of film to use, and where to place the cameras on the set.

Stephanie McMillan was the set decorator for the *Harry Potter* movies. Set decorator is another name for set designer.

# Set and Costume Designers

Besides cinematographers, there are many other important artists who work on movies. Set designers create drawings of scenery and props. They help create the story world that viewers see on the screen.

Costume designers plan the costumes, or clothes, characters wear in a movie. Sometimes costume designers pick the fabric, or cloth, and have costumes made. For other movies, the designer might rent costumes from a shop. One famous costume designer is Colleen Atwood. In 2004, she won an award, or honor, for the costumes in the movie *Lemony Snicket's A Series of Unfortunate Events*.

Rupert Grint (left), Daniel Radcliffe (middle), and Emma Watson (right) play Ron, Harry, and Hermione in the *Harry Potter* movies.

# Becoming Their Characters

Costumes help the actors in a movie bring their characters to life. An actor's most important job is to create interesting characters. By the time actors arrive on a set, they must know their lines, or the words their characters say. Then the cameras roll and the director says, "Action!" It is time for actors to play their characters!

Being an actor can be lots of fun. Daniel Radcliffe, the star of the *Harry Potter* movies, enjoyed meeting new friends on the set. However, he said that filming the Quidditch games was painful.

Actors Ben Stiller (left), David Schwimmer (middle), and Chris Rock (right) supplied voices for the animated movie *Madagascar*.

# Animated Movies

Not all movies have actors on-screen. Some movies, such as *Finding Nemo* and *Shrek*, are animated. Animated movies are made by showing pictures so quickly that they seem to move. Animated movies have dozens of pictures for each second. Actors record the voices of the drawn characters.

Some animated movies are made with hand-drawn animation. Artists draw millions of pictures by hand for these movies. In stop-motion animation, artists move and take pictures of objects, such as clay figures. Today many artists animate with computers. For example, the movie *Ratatouille* was made with 3-D computer animation.

Actors Jada Pinkett Smith (left), Will Smith (right), and Jaden Smith (front) appeared on the red carpet at the 2007 Academy Awards.

# Movie Events

When a new movie is ready for viewing, the producers want to call attention to it. They hold an event called a premiere, or first showing. Movie stars arrive at the theater to watch the movie and crowds gather outside to watch the stars.

Another important movie event is the Academy Awards. It honors the biggest accomplishments in movies each year. It opens with stars parading down the red **carpet**. Then, directors, actors, cinematographers, costume designers, and other people who work in movies win gold **statuettes**, known as Oscars, for their good work.

# Learning About Movies

If you want to be a moviemaker, there are things you can do now. Start by learning all you can about moviemaking. Watch movies and pay attention to music, sets, and props. When you get an idea for a story, write a screenplay. Find actors to play each character. If you can find a movie camera, film the scenes. Show your movie to family and friends.

Steven Spielberg, one of the greatest filmmakers of all time, spent his early years making movies just for fun. Now it is your turn to begin! Action!

# Glossary

**alien** (AY-lee-un)  A being from outer space.

**carpet** (KAHR-pet)  Rug.

**cinematographers** (sih-neh-muh-TO-gruh-ferz)  People in charge of the cameras, or tools that record scenes, in a movie.

**comics** (KO-miks)  Stories told mostly through drawings.

**create** (kree-AYT)  To produce or to make something.

**events** (ih-VENTS)  Things that happen.

**film** (FILM)  A strip of special matter on which pictures and movies are recorded.

**galaxy** (GA-lik-see)  A large group of stars and the worlds that circle them.

**sound effects** (SOWND if-FEKTS)  Sounds made by talented people for use in a movie.

**special effects** (SPEH-shul ih-FEKTS)  Parts of a movie that make scenes that are fake look real.

**statuettes** (sta-cheh-WETS)  Small figures of a person or animal.

**theaters** (THEE-uh-turz)  Buildings where plays and movies are shown.

# Index

# Web Sites

Due to the changing nature of Internet links, PowerKids Press has developed an online list of Web sites related to the subject of this book. This site is updated regularly. Please use this link to access the list:
www.powerkidslinks.com/djobs/movie/